D1364855

FIRST
LOOK IN

THE
FOREST

For a free color catalog describing Gareth Stevens' list of high-quality children's books, call 1-800-341-3569 (USA) or 1-800-461-9120 (Canada).

Library of Congress Cataloging-in-Publication Data

Butler, Daphne, 1945-
  [In the forest]
  First look in the forest / Daphne Butler.
      p. cm. -- (First look)
  Previously published as: In the forest. c1990.
  Includes bibliographical references and index.
  Summary: A simple introduction to forests and the life they contain.
  ISBN 0-8368-0506-2
  1. Forest ecology--Juvenile literature. 2. Forest fauna--Juvenile literature.
3. Forest flora--Juvenile literature. [1. Forest plants. 2. Forest animals.
3. Forest ecology. 4. Ecology.] I. Title. II. Series: Butler, Daphne, 1945- First look.
QH541.5.F6B87   1991
574.5'2642--dc20   90-10240

North American edition first published in 1991 by

Gareth Stevens Children's Books
1555 North RiverCenter Drive, Suite 201
Milwaukee, Wisconsin 53212, USA

U.S. edition copyright © 1991 by Gareth Stevens, Inc.   First published as *In the Forest* in
Great Britain, copyright © 1990, by Simon & Schuster Young Books. Additional end
matter copyright © 1991 by Gareth Stevens, Inc.

Photograph credits: Ardea, 12; Heather Angel, 11; ZEFA, all others
Drawings: Raymond Turvey

Series editor: Rita Reitci
Design: M&M Design Partnership
Cover design: Laurie Shock

Printed in the United States of America

1 2 3 4 5 6 7 8 9 97 96 95 94 93 92 91

FIRST LOOK IN

THE FOREST

DAPHNE BUTLER

Gareth Stevens Children's Books
MILWAUKEE

Books in the
FIRST LOOK series:

CONTENTS

FORESTS ARE WILD PLACES

In the forest you may find many kinds of plants, animals, and trees.

If you have ever been in the forest, can you remember what it was like?

7

FOREST PLANTS GROW IN MANY WAYS

As you walk through the forest, notice the differences in the trees and plants. They may grow better in some places than in others.

Sometimes the undergrowth is so thick that you can't walk through it, and you have to find your way around.

9

STOP AND LISTEN

Can you hear birds singing, or the wind rustling in the trees? Perhaps you can hear water gurgling in a stream.

The sounds change in other parts of the forest.

11

ANIMALS IN THE FOREST

If you stand still and keep quiet, you may see forest animals and birds.

Here they make their homes. Among forest trees and plants, they can find food and a safe place to have their babies.

NEW LEAVES

Many forest trees have bare branches in winter because their leaves died and fell off in autumn. New leaves grow when it gets warmer in spring.

Trees that do this are called deciduous trees.

15

16

FOREST FLOWERS

Between the trees, flowers grow in the warm spring sunshine.

Later, in summer, the trees will have many big leaves that shade the ground. It may even be too shady for flowers to grow.

THICK EVERGREEN LEAVES

Trees that have leaves all year long are called evergreen trees.

Holly is one of the evergreens in the forest. It grows red berries that birds eat during the winter.

19

MANY FORESTS ARE OLD

It takes a long time for trees to grow big. Many live for hundreds of years.

Each year, a tree grows another layer of wood, called a growth ring. The trunk is the oldest part of the tree, and it has the most growth rings.

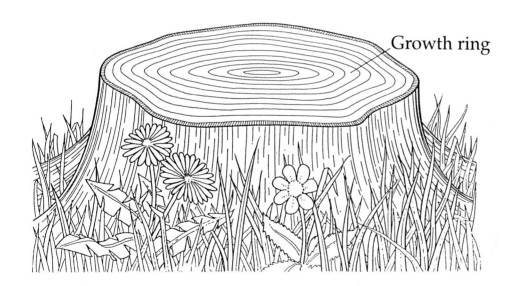

Growth ring

21

22

CONIFERS

A conifer is a tree with needles instead of leaves, and cones instead of fruit. The oldest living tree on Earth is a conifer.

There are many different conifers in forests. Most of them are evergreens that have needles on their branches all year long.

KEEP THE FOREST CLEAN

You might see trash left in the forest. Trash is unsightly and can be dangerous for the animals.

Some kinds of trash can poison trees and kill them.

LISTEN TO A NEW SOUND

You might hear a chain saw buzzing loudly as a worker cuts down trees nearby.

Why do you think the worker is cutting down the trees?

27

FIRE!

Fire can be very dangerous in the forest, so you must always be careful when you use it.

In a dry summer, wind can blow fire from tree to tree and burn down a large section of the forest.

When a forest burns, what happens to the animals that live there?

More Books about the Forest

Animals of the Forest. Mora (Barron's Educational Series)
Explore a Tropical Forest (2 volumes). Crump (National Geographic)
Fire! in Yellowstone. Ekey (Gareth Stevens)
Forest Ranger. Pellowski (Troll)
The Hidden Life of the Forest. Kuhn (Crown)
Life in the Forest. Curran (Troll)
Our Changing World: The Forest. Bellamy (Crown)
Rain Forest. Coucher (Farrar, Straus & Giroux)
Tree Trunk Traffic. Lavies (Dutton)
Trees. Gordon (Troll)
Trees. Langley (Franklin Watts)
Wonders of the Forest. Sabin (Troll)
Woods and Forests. Cuisin (Silver)

Glossary

Autumn: The season that comes between summer and winter. It is also called fall. In autumn, plants stop growing, and many of them lose their green color. Leaves turn color and fall from trees. Days begin to get shorter and colder. Some animals travel to warmer areas. Other animals gather food and make homes where they will spend the winter.

Conifers: Evergreen trees that have cones. Each year, conifers grow seeds inside cones, instead of inside fruit like some other trees. Then the cones drop off and the seeds later fall out on the ground. Animals and birds eat most of the seeds, but some grow into new evergreen trees. The oldest tree that is still living is a bristlecone pine. This conifer is over 4,700 years old!

Deciduous trees: Trees that shed, or drop, their leaves every year. Their leaves are usually flat and broad. They often turn color in the autumn.

Evergreen trees: Trees that stay green all year long. Most of them have needles, but some of them have broad leaves. Many evergreens are conifers, but some evergreens are not. Holly is an example of an evergreen that is not a conifer.

Forest: A thick growth of trees and plants that covers a very large area. A forest is larger than woods.

Growth ring: A layer of wood that a tree grows in one year. These layers look like rings after a tree is cut down. You can tell how old a tree is by counting the rings in its trunk. Measuring the trunk of a living tree can help tell its age.

Needles: Short, narrow pointed leaves that stay on a tree all year long. Needles grow on evergreen trees. They do not change color in the autumn.

Spring: The time of year between winter and summer. In spring, plants begin to grow. Leaves come out on the trees. The days become longer and warmer. Many animals have babies in the spring.

Trash: Anything that people throw away, such as garbage and empty containers. Trash thrown into the forest can be harmful. Animals can get cut from opened cans. Plastic straps and rings can trap animals and birds by their feet or their necks and cause them to die. Some kinds of trash can damage or poison the ground so that plants and trees cannot grow. Trash can pollute streams and ponds. Trash is unsightly and destroys the beauty for people who visit forests.

Undergrowth: The small trees, shrubs, and other plants that grow beneath large trees in woods or forests. Undergrowth is also called underbrush.

Index

A number that is in **boldface** type means that the page has a picture of the subject on it.